SUPER CITIES!

DETROIT

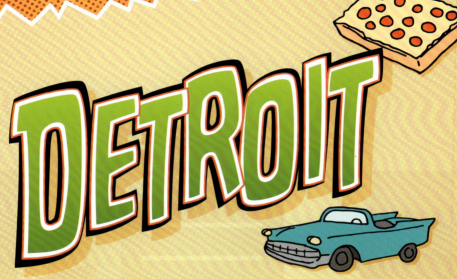

by **Daralynn Walker**

arcadia
CHILDREN'S BOOKS

Published by Arcadia Children's Books
A Division of Arcadia Publishing
Charleston, SC
www.arcadiapublishing.com

Copyright © 2023 by Arcadia Children's Books
All rights reserved

Super Cities is a trademark of Arcadia Publishing, Inc.

First published 2023

Manufactured in the United States of America.

ISBN 978-1-4671-9897-4

Library of Congress Control Number: 2022950472

Notice: The information in this book is true and complete to the best of our knowledge. It is offered without guarantee on the part of the author or Arcadia Publishing. The author and Arcadia Publishing disclaim all liability in connection with the use of this book.

All rights reserved. No part of this book may be reproduced or transmitted in any form whatsoever without prior written permission from the publisher except in the case of brief quotations embodied in critical articles and reviews.

Produced by Shoreline Publishing Group LLC
Santa Barbara, California
Designer: Patty Kelley
Production: Steve Scheluchin

Contents

Welcome to Detroit!.................. 4
Detroit: Map it!..................... 6
A City on Wheels.................... 8
Detroit Means 10
Rolling on the River 12
History: Early Days 14
History: City of War 16
History: The Underground Railroad . 18
History: Boomtown.................. 20
History: A City of Firsts 22
Civil Rights in Detroit.............. 24
Detroit Grows Up................... 28
Detroit Today 30
The Motown Sound................. 32
Detroit's Musical Heroes 34
Things to See 36
Museums: Go See 'Em 38
The Spirit of Detroit 42
Detroit Weather 44
Getting Around Detroit............ 46
It's Official!........................ 48

Canada: A Bridge Away 50
Outdoor Art in Detroit............. 52
Art in Museums 54
How to Talk Detroit................ 56
Detroit: It's Weird!................. 58
Famous People Today 60
What People Do In Detroit......... 62
Go, Detroit Sports.................. 64
Detroit: College Town 70
Eat the Detroit Way 72
Detroit Street Quiz!................ 74
We Saw It at the Zoo 76
Animals in Detroit................. 78
Belle Isle: The Jewel of Detroit 80
Spooky Sites 82
Detroit by the Numbers 84
Not Far Away 86
Sister Cities 90
Find Out More 92
Index............................. 94

WELCOME TO Detroit!

Detroit, Michigan

When you hear the name Detroit, what comes to mind? Cars! Motown music! Lots of sports teams! And it's north of Canada! Of course, those are just a few of the great things about this historic and busy Midwestern city. In this book, you'll learn all about those things, plus many more reasons to visit Detroit!

Why cars? Since cars started rolling in the early 1900s, Detroit has been home to some of the biggest carmakers in America. Ford, Chrysler, and General Motors are known as "The Big 3." The auto industry has spread around the world, but Detroit remains America's vroom-vroom center.

Motown is a nickname for Detroit, but it's also the name of a fantastic type of music that was very popular in the 1960s.

FAST FACTS
Detroit, Michigan
POPULATION: 661,193
METRO DETROIT POPULATION: 4,392,041
FOUNDED: July 24, 1701
NICKNAMES: Motown, Motor City, Hockeytown USA

The Motown sound was among the first to combine Black musical traditions with pop songs. Even now, you can still hear Motown's pop-influenced style in a lot of songs.

Why sports? Few American cities can boast top teams in all four of the major sports. Also, Detroit is "Hockeytown USA"!

Wait, wait . . . the food! People in Detroit love their Coney Dogs and their Vernors ginger ale!

There is so much more, including dozens of great places to see and things to do. Plus, there have been many inventions, businesses, and ideas born in Detroit, and almost anything can be built here. This book will show you why Detroit is such a great city, full of stories of success, courage, and strength. Let's go!

Detroit 5

DETROIT: Map It!

Detroit is the largest city in Michigan, located in the southeastern part of the state. It has a major port on the Detroit River, which connects small Lake St. Clair with huge Lake Erie. The Detroit River also connects Detroit to Canada on the south and was once one of the busiest shipping districts in the world. Unlike most of the United States, Detroit is north of part of Canada. There are three ways to get from Canada to Detroit: a highway tunnel, a railway tunnel, and the Ambassador Bridge. This is the second busiest border crossing in North America.

State flower, the apple blossom

6 Detroit

A City on Wheels

The first cars in America were invented and built in the late 1800s. By the early 1900s, automobile factories were sprouting up everywhere, but Detroit quickly became the national center. A man named Ransom Olds came first in 1897, and then Henry Ford started his company here in 1901. General Motors was founded in 1908. By then, Detroit was officially the Motor City and everyone wanted to be a part of the action.

1897: The new Olds Motor Vehicle Company had 11 vehicle types for sale by 1901.

1901: Henry Ford's company really kickstarted the car business and brought people from all over the world to work in the auto industry.

Detroit

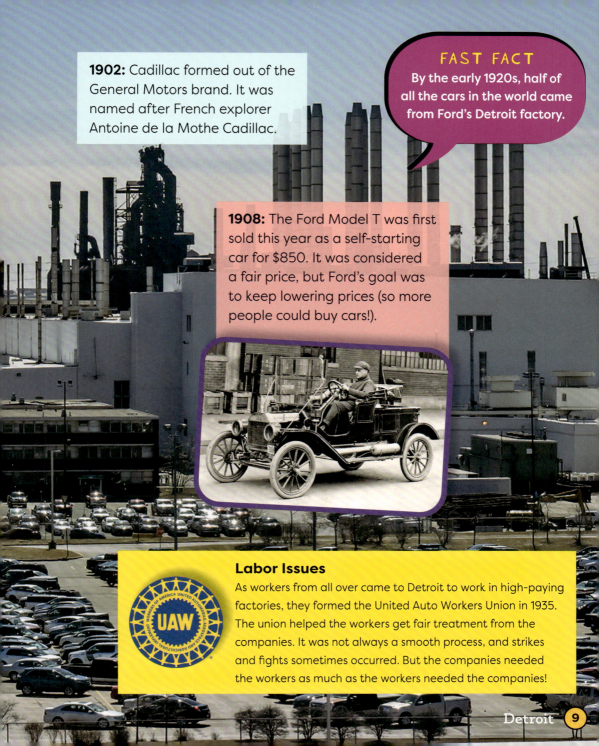

1902: Cadillac formed out of the General Motors brand. It was named after French explorer Antoine de la Mothe Cadillac.

FAST FACT
By the early 1920s, half of all the cars in the world came from Ford's Detroit factory.

1908: The Ford Model T was first sold this year as a self-starting car for $850. It was considered a fair price, but Ford's goal was to keep lowering prices (so more people could buy cars!).

Labor Issues

As workers from all over came to Detroit to work in high-paying factories, they formed the United Auto Workers Union in 1935. The union helped the workers get fair treatment from the companies. It was not always a smooth process, and strikes and fights sometimes occurred. But the companies needed the workers as much as the workers needed the companies!

Detroit 9

DETROIT MEANS...

The first European settlers to live in Detroit were French explorers who were looking for precious metals and new routes to travel to Asia (page 16). As they traveled west from the French-Canadian city of Montreal, they reached the site of modern-day Detroit. In June 1701, French explorer Antoine Laumet de la Mothe Cadillac claimed the land as Fort Pontchartrain Du Detroit. Soldiers and Native American guides came with him in 25 boats, and they were amazed by Detroit's rich soil and great amount of natural resources.

In English, we say the city's name as "deh-TROYT." But the name comes from the French word *détroit*, which is pronounced "deh-TWAH" and means "strait," a fancy word for a narrow waterway. So that makes sense, since the Detroit River helps connects Lake Erie on the south with Lake Huron on the north. Cadillac quickly began construction on the fort after he and his men arrived.

Cadillac's family crest

If Cadillac came back, he'd see this statue of himself in Detroit.

Detroit 11

Rolling on the River

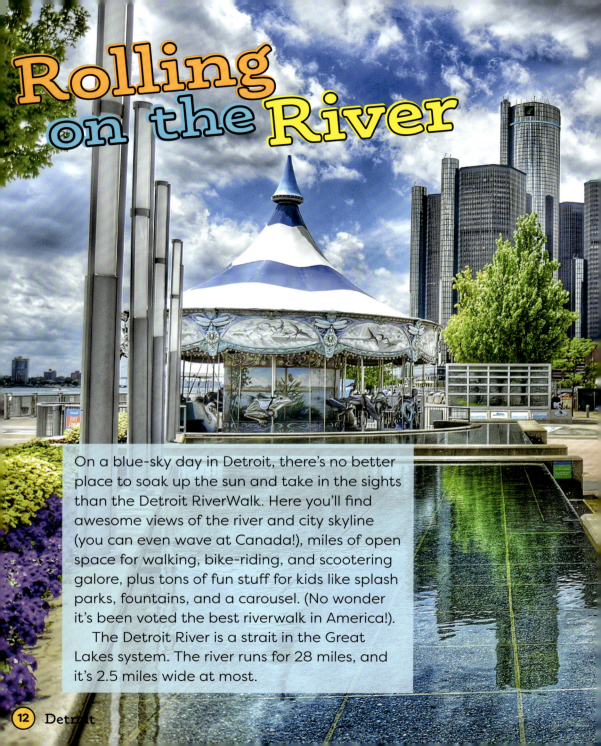

On a blue-sky day in Detroit, there's no better place to soak up the sun and take in the sights than the Detroit RiverWalk. Here you'll find awesome views of the river and city skyline (you can even wave at Canada!), miles of open space for walking, bike-riding, and scootering galore, plus tons of fun stuff for kids like splash parks, fountains, and a carousel. (No wonder it's been voted the best riverwalk in America!).

The Detroit River is a strait in the Great Lakes system. The river runs for 28 miles, and it's 2.5 miles wide at most.

HISTORY: Early Days

First People: By the beginning of the 1600s, there were more than 90,000 Indigenous peoples living along the Detroit River, including the Ojibwe, Ottawa, and Potawatomi people. During the fall and winter, these groups hunted, trapped, and skinned animals.

New Arrivals: When Antoine de la Mothe Cadillac came to the area in 1701 (page 10), relations were friendly at first. The Indigenous peoples had leather, beaver skins, sable, and fox furs to trade for muskets, knives, hatchets, and clothes. They also taught the new arrivals how to make maple sugar, find honey, and gather fruits, root vegetables, and nuts. As more settlers came, there were more arguments about land, prices, and how to trade goods, among other things. The people who lived in Detroit first began to worry about the Europeans.

14 Detroit

Here Comes War: Relations between Indigenous peoples and French settlers got worse as the French tried to add taxes or did not trade fairly. Things turned violent. In 1712, Indigenous peoples destroyed most of the French fort at Detroit.

Seven Years' War: The French continued to control Detroit and what would become Michigan, but Great Britain wanted the land, too. Starting in 1756, French colonists joined with Indigenous peoples to fight off a British invasion in what was also called the French and Indian War.

HISTORY: City of War

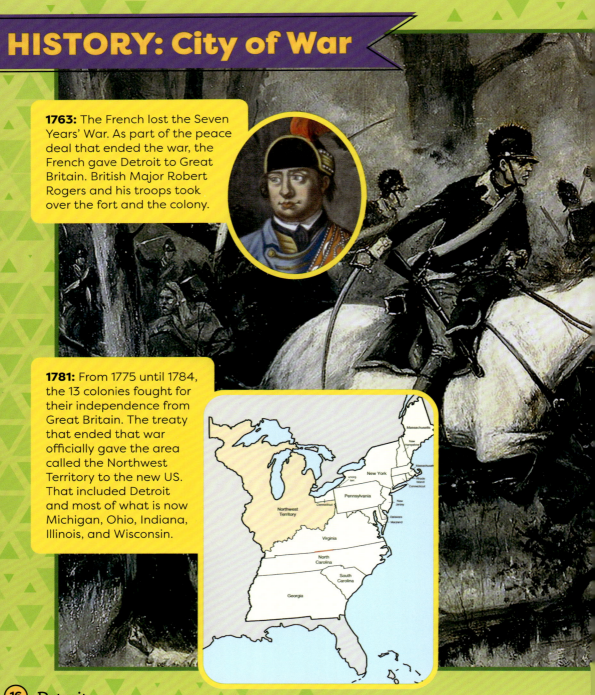

1763: The French lost the Seven Years' War. As part of the peace deal that ended the war, the French gave Detroit to Great Britain. British Major Robert Rogers and his troops took over the fort and the colony.

1781: From 1775 until 1784, the 13 colonies fought for their independence from Great Britain. The treaty that ended that war officially gave the area called the Northwest Territory to the new US. That included Detroit and most of what is now Michigan, Ohio, Indiana, Illinois, and Wisconsin.

Detroit

1794: The British did not leave Detroit completely until 1794. That year, President George Washington sent General Anthony Wayne to drive the British out. At the Battle of the Fallen Timbers, Wayne's American army won and the British left.

June 11, 1805: The Great Fire of Detroit ripped through the wooden structures of the city, burning everything to the ground, except for one building. After the destruction, Augustus B. Woodward, a territory official, formed a street plan that looked like the spokes of a wheel. This plan was based on the layout of Washington, DC.

FAST FACT

The Detroit flag was made after the 1805 fire. On it is Detroit's motto: "Speramus Meliora: Resurget Cinerbus." It's in Latin and means, "We hope for better things; it will rise from the ashes."

Detroit

HISTORY: The Underground Railroad

Until the end of the Civil War (1865), slavery was legal in southern states. (Michigan was a free state.) But starting in the 1830s, abolitionists (people against slavery) created a secret system of places where escaped enslaved people could hide as they made their way to freedom in northern states and Canada.

This system of safe places, called "stations"—and the guides, or "conductors," who helped—was called the Underground Railroad. Detroit played a key role.

There was no paper map to the Railroad, so people traveling had to use maps sewn into quilts, directions hidden in songs, and the shapes of the stars. Conductors provided travel to folks escaping to the north, and "Station Masters" provided food and shelter. Detroit was the last stop before Canada.

1833: The Blackburns, an enslaved couple on the run, were helped by Detroit's Black community to flee to Canada, resulting in the city's first race riot. The anti-slavery campaign in Detroit begins with this incident.

1836: The Second Baptist Church was founded by thirteen formerly enslaved people. It was the first African American Baptist congregation and an important part of Detroit's Underground Railroad.

Detroit

FAST FACT
The Underground Railroad code name for Detroit was "Midnight."

1837: Robert Banks, William Lambert, and Madison J. Lightfoot formed the Detroit Anti-Slavery Society. The Society not only wanted slavery to end, but also wanted "our Black brothers to be raised to their rightful place as men."

1840s: Over the course of nearly 30 years, more than 45,000 people passed through Detroit on their way to Canada.

Conductors in Detroit

Seymour Finney: He was owner of the Finney Hotel and used his stable to hide freedom seekers.

George De Baptiste: A prominent business owner, he bought a steam boat to smuggle a large number of people on the Detroit River to Canada.

William Lambert: He was one of the wealthiest Black men in Detroit at the time. He bought 40 wagons that had secret compartments built in them to carry people from the South to freedom.

Seymour Finney

William Lambert

Detroit

HISTORY: Boomtown

1850s: The Port of Detroit helped the city become a top shipping gateway to the United States. More than 150 steamboats were constructed at the port. These were used to carry copper, ore, and other raw materials.

1860s: Detroit organized its first police department, opened a public library, and founded Wayne State University. Detroit was developing and emerging as one of the largest cities in the Midwest.

1861-65: The Civil War was fought between the Union in the North and the Confederate States in the South. The main issue was the future of slavery in the United States. The Union won and slavery was banned for good. No battles were fought in Michigan during the Civil War, but the soldiers of the Michigan 24th Infantry fought hard for the Union. This regiment was formed in August 1862 and was part of the "Iron Brigade."

Surprise Soda

According to the story, Vernors was invented during the Civil War! James Vernor, who worked in a pharmacy and soda shop, was trying out different kinds of ginger ale drinks. He left a barrel of ginger ale in an oak barrel while he went to fight in the war. When he got back, the mixture had turned into the tasty drink that people in Detroit know and love today.

James Vernor

Elijah McCoy

1872: Elijah McCoy, a Black inventor from Detroit, patented the first automatic lubricating cup for steam locomotives. This key invention helped steam engines work more safely and helped the railroad industry grow.

1889: The first skyscraper in Detroit, the Hammond Building, was built. Ten stories high, the structure had lower floors made of stone and brick. The building had 246 offices as well as shops on the ground floor.

Detroit 21

HISTORY: City of Firsts

Detroit was and is filled with innovative people. As an emerging city in the late 1800s, Detroit was on the frontier of creating new and exciting things. Here are just a few:

1896: Charles Brady King was the first person in Detroit to drive a motor vehicle. It was the first car to ever drive on the streets of Detroit.

1909: Woodward Avenue (named after Augustus B. Woodward, page 17) became the first mile of concrete road in the country. At the time the project cost about $14,000, which would be about $2 million today.

1913: The first automotive assembly line was developed in Detroit by Henry Ford. His idea to put cars together on an assembly line helped increase production. Ford was inspired by conveyor belts used at Chicago meatpacking plants.

1920: The first radio station to be owned by a newspaper was in Detroit. First known as 8MK, it's still in business as WWJ. When it started, it reached just 30 homes, but put Detroit on the map.

1939: Detroit was home to the first urban freeway. It consisted of six lanes and helped increase the flow of traffic.

New Arrivals

From 1910 to 1930, the population of Detroit increased from 466,000 to 1.56 million people. Three-quarters of the population were immigrants from other countries or were part of the Great Migration. That was the movement of Black Americans from the South to northern states, seeking better jobs and higher wages in industrial cities.

Detroit 23

HISTORY: The Late 1900s

In 1950, Detroit was a busy city with a population of over 1.8 million people.

1959: Berry Gordy founded Motown. Detroit-born artists like Diana Ross and the Temptations helped make the city a center of popular music in America.

1963: Dr. Martin Luther King participated in the "Walk to Freedom" in 1963 in Detroit. In June 1963, 125,000 people marched down Woodward Avenue in Detroit in support of Civil Rights. At the time, this was the largest Civil Rights march in US history.

1967: One of the worst riots in US history started on 12th Street in a Black neighborhood. It started when residents reacted to a police raid. Fighting began and spread over many blocks. After five days, 43 people were killed, 342 were hurt, and 1,400 buildings were burned.

1968: The Detroit Tigers won the World Series, defeating the St. Louis Cardinals. (They won again in 1984!)

24 Detroit

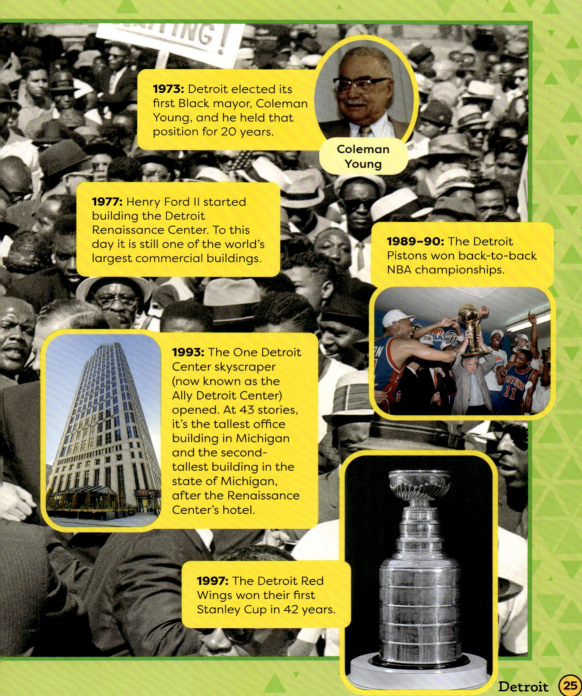

1973: Detroit elected its first Black mayor, Coleman Young, and he held that position for 20 years.

Coleman Young

1977: Henry Ford II started building the Detroit Renaissance Center. To this day it is still one of the world's largest commercial buildings.

1989–90: The Detroit Pistons won back-to-back NBA championships.

1993: The One Detroit Center skyscraper (now known as the Ally Detroit Center) opened. At 43 stories, it's the tallest office building in Michigan and the second-tallest building in the state of Michigan, after the Renaissance Center's hotel.

1997: The Detroit Red Wings won their first Stanley Cup in 42 years.

Detroit

People from the Past!

Meet some interesting people from Detroit's past.

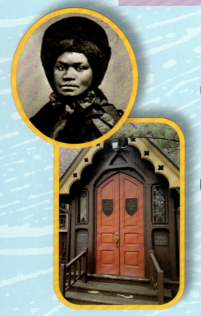

Elizabeth Forth (1786–1866)

When Elizabeth Forth was born, Michigan was not yet a state. Despite slavery being illegal in the Northwest Territory, some groups still enslaved people. Elizabeth was born an enslaved person near Detroit, but when she grew up, she became free after escaping to Canada. She returned and became the first Black property owner in Oakland County. She bought 48 acres in what is now Pontiac, a suburb of Detroit. She used the money from her estate to build the St. James Episcopal Church Denison in Grosse Isle, a nearby town, so that people from all walks of life could worship together. The church is still open today.

Joe Louis (1914–1981)

Louis was an American boxer known as "the Brown Bomber," and considered one of the best and most influential boxers of all time. Louis moved to Detroit with his family in 1926. He was the world heavyweight champion for 12 years, from 1937 until 1949. He won his title 25 times in a row, which is a record for all weight classes. Louis held the title of champion longer than any other boxer in history.

Rosa Parks (1913–2005)

Rosa Parks was a Civil Rights activist who is best known for her key role in the Montgomery bus boycott, which started in 1955 after she was arrested for refusing to give up her bus seat to a white person in Montgomery, Alabama. Not long after, Parks moved to Detroit, where she remained active in the fight for Civil Rights until she died in the city in 2005. Congress has recognized her as "the first lady of Civil Rights" and "the mother of the freedom movement."

Malcolm X (1925–1965)

Born Malcolm Little, Malcolm X was a prominent voice in the Civil Rights Movement and a leader in the Nation of Islam until 1964. He spent a lot of time in and near Detroit when he was a teenager, and became involved with the Nation in the city in his 20s. He ran one of the Nation's temples there and made several of his most important speeches in Detroit. Malcolm X was killed by gunmen in New York City in 1965.

Detroit Today

The population of Detroit peaked at 1.8 million in 1950 and has shrunk ever since. One reason for that is that many people moved out of the city to nearby suburbs. However, Detroit remains an important city in America.

Music: Detroit is known for Motown and Techno Music. Motown was founded in Detroit and has been a staple since its inception in 1959. Techno Music has made its way around the world and back to Detroit. Every year Detroit hosts a three-day festival that brings out the biggest names in the music business!

Food: If you want good food, come to Detroit. The famous Detroit-style pizza has a thick, crispy, and chewy crust that is baked with the pepperoni right in it! Coney Dogs (hot dogs topped with chili, chopped onions, and mustard) are amazing, and don't forget about our world famous Vernors ginger ale!

Detroit

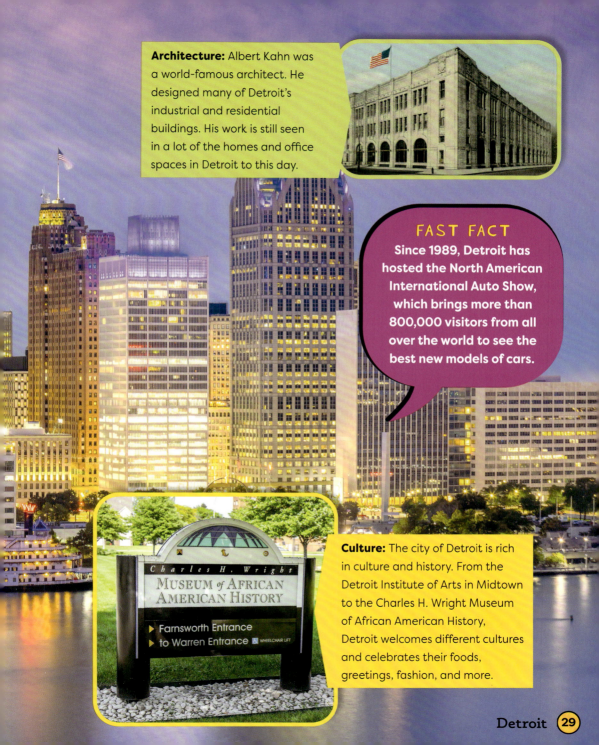

Architecture: Albert Kahn was a world-famous architect. He designed many of Detroit's industrial and residential buildings. His work is still seen in a lot of the homes and office spaces in Detroit to this day.

FAST FACT
Since 1989, Detroit has hosted the North American International Auto Show, which brings more than 800,000 visitors from all over the world to see the best new models of cars.

Culture: The city of Detroit is rich in culture and history. From the Detroit Institute of Arts in Midtown to the Charles H. Wright Museum of African American History, Detroit welcomes different cultures and celebrates their foods, greetings, fashion, and more.

Detroit 29

The Motown Sound

In the late 1950s, Berry Gordy, Jr., started a Detroit music company that celebrated Black artists who mixed soul music and rhythm and blues with pop music. This sound was hugely popular throughout the 1960s and 1970s, and still influences artists today. Motown's artists and businesspeople achieved national and international fame at a time when Black people were fighting for Civil Rights.

January 12, 1959: Berry Gordy, Jr., opened Tamla Records and signed his first recording artist in the same year. The company changed its name to Motown later that year, a play on the Motor City nickname. (Motor Town, get it?) Gordy purchased Motown's Detroit headquarters and nicknamed it "Hitsville, U.S.A."

1960: The Miracles, the first group signed by Gordy, earned national recognition for their hit "Shop Around."

1964: "My Guy" by Mary Wells became Motown's fourth number-one single on the Billboard Hot 100 and the label's first major hit in the United Kingdom. This song briefly beat the Beatles for a few weeks.

1967: Gladys Knight & the Pips' "I Heard It Through the Grapevine" reaches No. 2 on the pop charts.

1969: The Jackson 5 signs with Motown, launching the five Jackson brothers into the spotlight. You may have heard of the youngest brother, Michael (who was just 10 years old at the time), who went on to have an extraordinary career.

1971: Motown won its second Grammy Award for Dr. Martin Luther King, Jr.'s. recording of his speech, "Why I Oppose the War in Vietnam"

1972: Motown artist Stevie Wonder kicked off his 50-date tour opening for the Rolling Stones—one of the world's most successful bands.

FAST FACT
Michael Jackson debuted his "moonwalk" for the world during the "Motown: 25" show.

1978: Motown released "The Wiz," an adaptation of "The Wizard of Oz" starring Diana Ross, Michael Jackson, and Richard Pryor, among other important Black artists.

1983: The two hour TV special, "Motown: 25," featured performances from The Jackson 5, Diana Ross, The Four Tops, and more.

Detroit 31

Detroit's Musical Heroes

Alice Cooper The career of this American rock singer spans more than 54 years. He is a Detroit native whose real name is Vincent Damon Furnier!

Stevie Wonder is an American singer and songwriter and one of the most popular musicians of all time. He moved to Detroit when he was four years old. Though he is blind, he was a star singer and harmonica player by the time he was 11. Later, his use of electronic instruments in the 1970s changed R&B music. Wonder has sold more than 100 million records all over the world and won 25 Grammys. He's the only Grammy-winner to win five or more awards on one night—three times!.

Aretha Franklin The Queen of Soul was born and raised in Detroit. Some of her most popular hits were "Respect," "Think," "Amazing Grace," and "Chain of Fools." In 2008, *Rolling Stone* ranked her first among the "100 Greatest Singers of All Time."

Diana Ross Launched to fame as the lead singer of The Supremes, who were Motown's most popular group in the 1960s, and one of the best-selling girl groups of all time. She was later an international singing star on her own, winning four Grammys as well as Lifetime Achievement honors at the BET Music Awards in 2007, Grammy Awards in 2012, and American Music Awards in 2017.

Detroit 33

34 Detroit

Here are some cool places to visit if you ever find your way to Detroit. These are loved by locals and tourists alike.

Renaissance Center

General Motors owns the Renaissance Center complex on the Detroit International Riverfront as its world headquarters. Since its completion in 1977, the central tower has been the tallest structure in Michigan, at 727 feet. One of the seven towers houses the Detroit Marriott Renaissance Hotel, which has 73 stories of hotel rooms, banquet halls, retail, and more. The total area of the complex is 5.5 million square feet. Tourists enjoy visiting the restaurant at the top of the Renaissance Center or simply admiring the view of the Detroit River and the Windsor, Ontario, skyline.

Fisher Building

This 30-story building is located in the heart of the New Center Area and was designed by world-renowned architect Albert Kahn. Come see a Broadway play in the theater, or visit one of the retail stores on the ground floor for some Detroit memorabilia. This National Historic Landmark is known as "Detroit's Largest Art Object."

Things to See in Detroit

Monument to Joe Louis: The sculpture of the bronze arm of heavyweight boxing champion Joe Louis (page 26)—24 feet long and 5,000 pounds—was given to the city in 1986. Some think it honors Louis's 1938 knockout win over German boxer Max Schmeling, which was an emotional victory against Nazi Germany.

Campus Martius Park: After the Great Fire of 1805, Detroit was rebuilt with a new city plan. Augustus B. Woodward placed this park at the center of that plan. It remains a centerpiece today, a place to relax on a beach in the middle of Detroit. Locals take their lunch breaks outside in this area, where food trucks often gather. There are hundreds of free concerts, festivals, and family-friendly activities here. There's even an ice rink in winter.

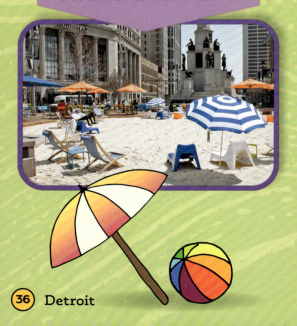

Hart Plaza: Said to be the site where Cadillac started the first settlement in Detroit, it's home to the RiverWalk, a 3.5-mile path along the Detroit riverfront. Every year, thousands of people go to Hart Plaza to see concerts in the two outdoor theaters, where shows are usually held in warmer months.

36 Detroit

Underground Railroad Sites

Gateway to Freedom: Several routes of the Underground Railroad (page 18) ran through Michigan. That history is honored by this sculpture on the Detroit riverfront. It shows six freedom seekers getting ready to board a boat to Canada. The man pointing from Detroit to Windsor is George DeBaptiste, who lived in Detroit and was a conductor on the Underground Railroad. He helped enslaved people cross the river to freedom. A matching monument in Windsor shows a person raising his arms to celebrate his freedom while a Quaker woman helps a woman and her child.

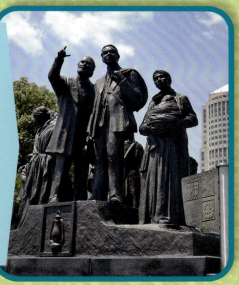

Second Baptist Church: An Underground Railroad station was in the basement of the Second Baptist Church, in the area of Detroit now called Greektown. The street where the church stands today was named after Rev. William C. Monroe, the church's conductor on the Underground Railroad. About 5,000 freedom seekers sought safety in the basement here.

Detroit

Museums— Go See 'Em!

Find out more about all sorts of Detroit-y things in this collection of museums and historical sites!

Dossin Great Lakes Museum This historical maritime museum on Belle Isle has one of the world's largest collections of model ships. It also has displays about the history and ships of the Great Lakes. Want to see one of the fastest hydroplane racing boats of all time? It's at the Dossin.

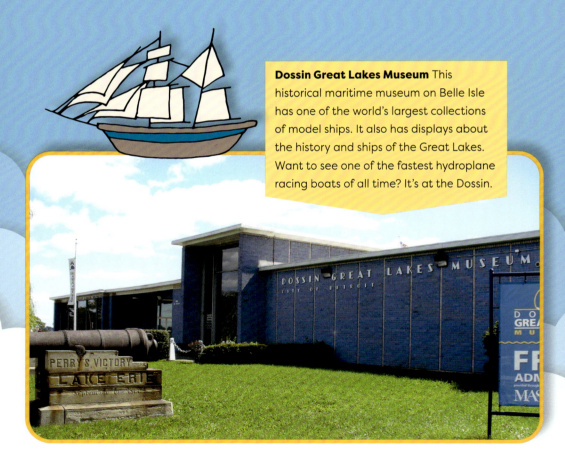

Detroit

Motown Museum If you like the Motown sound, you should go to Hitsville U.S.A., which was Motown's first home and recording studio. The house was bought in 1959, and it has costumes, pictures, and records from some of Motown's best-known artists. You will see the original instruments and sheet music for famous songs like "My Girl" that are known all over the world.

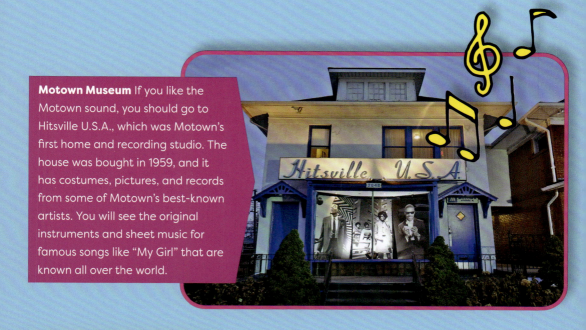

Eastern Market People from around the world come to see this famous Farmers Market. Since it opened in 1891, the market has grown from hosting small farmers downtown to the largest historical public market district in the United States, covering 43 acres. People from all over the state come to sell their fresh fruits, vegetables, breads, and other goods.

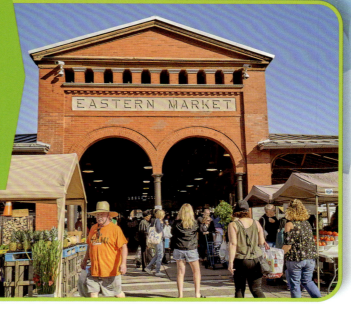

Detroit 39

More Museums!

Detroit Historical Museum The Detroit Historical Museum is right in the middle of Midtown. It has more than three floors of exhibits about Detroit's past and present. In the basement, there is a cool recreation of old Detroit, complete with cobblestone streets and shops that take you back in time.

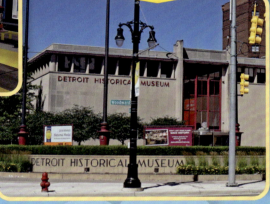

Charles H. Wright Museum of African American History When you enter this historic structure, the 55-foot-tall glass dome will be the first thing that catches your eye. Opened in 1965, this was the first museum in Detroit to focus on the Black experience. It has rotating exhibits that show Detroit's Black history and life.

Michigan Science Center Do you like big magnets, robots, and science experiments that you can do with your hands? Then you should go to the Science Center. Located in Midtown right across the street from the Detroit Institute of Arts, it has more than 200 interactive exhibits for both kids and adults. They also throw the best Halloween parties here!

Henry Ford Greenfield Village Located west of downtown Detroit, this is the place to go if you want to ride in a Model T car, walk through early 1800s neighborhoods, or take a pottery class. In a place founded by Henry Ford and featuring his collections from American history, homes from the early days of America have been reconstructed on more than 80 acres in Greenfield Village.

Detroit

Spirit of Detroit

People from all over the world recognize this famous 20-foot-tall figure. *The Spirit of Detroit* sculpture has been on the edge of downtown near Woodward for more than 60 years. It was sculpted by Marshall Fredericks, a world famous artist. Known as a skillful sculptor, his legacy will always be the bronze "Green Giant" that celebrates the pride and resilience of Detroit.

Fredericks did not initially name the sculpture; the citizens of Detroit chose the name based on an inscription from a verse in the Bible, now carved on the marble wall behind it. "Now, the Lord is that Spirit, and wherever the Spirit of the Lord is, there is liberty."

Detroit

When the *Spirit of Detroit* is decked out in sports jerseys to support local teams who make it to the playoffs, it serves as a representation of the hard work those athletes put in! It has frequently worn jerseys for Detroit Tigers baseball and Detroit Red Wings hockey.

Detroit 43

Detroit Weather

Everyone knows that winters in Detroit can be very cold and windy, but no one ever mentions how wonderful and pleasant the summers are! With more than 180 days of sunshine per year, there are plenty of days when the city is sunny and breezy!

Four Season State! Summers in Detroit are warm; winters are cold, snowy, and windy; and it is partly cloudy all year. Spring is wet and rainy, and autumn is cool and crisp, but you always get four seasons! April has the lowest humidity while December has the highest.

Snow Storms Galore: Every year, about 33 inches of snow fall in Detroit. "Lake effect" snow is a common cause of heavy snowstorms in Michigan. Those storms happen when cold air from the north moves across the open waters of the Great Lakes. As that cold air travels, heat and moisture are transferred to the lowest part of the atmosphere, making for fast-moving snowstorms.

Best Time to Visit: The best time to visit Detroit is between late spring and early fall. This is the warmest time of the year. The busiest months for tourists are June, July, and August.

GETTING AROUND DETROIT

Detroit didn't get the nickname "Motor City" for nothing. Since the early 1900s Detroiters have used cars as their main mode of transportation, but as the years progressed more and more options to get around have become available. Let's check them out!

Buses: The Detroit Department of Transportation provides bus service throughout the city, with stops at or near most major attractions. It has several routes that run around the clock so you can see Detroit day or night!

Bikes: MoGo is the city's bike share program. Stations are spread throughout downtown, allowing you to borrow and return any of the bicycles easily. Explore the city of Detroit by bicycle for an affordable price!

46 Detroit

The People Mover: These trains zip around the downtown area. There are 13 People Mover stations. Taking the train is a convenient and safe way to get around town for the whole family. Most people in the area use the People Mover to go to sports events or concerts. Others use it to see the sights, and some use it every day to get to work.

The Qline: Between downtown Detroit and Grand Boulevard, the QLine streetcar system serves downtown parks, theaters, arenas, colleges, museums, and businesses. The QLine was originally known as M-1 Rail by its creators, and runs along historic Woodward Avenue.

IT'S OFFICIAL!

All towns have their favorite official stuff. These items tell you everything great about a city. Here are a few official things for Detroit and the state of Michigan.

OFFICIAL CITY FLAG:
The flag has been changed a few times, but the most recent flag has four sections that represent countries—France, Great Britain, and the United States—that have controlled Detroit. In the middle is a seal which shows a picture of the Great Fire of 1805. The figure on the left weeps while the figure on the right has hopes for a new city to rise.

CITY SYMBOL:
The Spirit of Detroit is used widely as a symbol on police logos and government buildings.

Detroit

FLOWER: Apple blossom

STONE: Petoskey stone

OFFICIAL MICHIGAN STATE STUFF

Nickname:
Wolverine State

State Tree:
Towering white pine

FISH: trout

BIRD: American Robin

Detroit 49

Canada: A Bridge Away

Directly south of Detroit is another country: Canada! Connecting the two nations is the Ambassador Bridge, the world's longest international suspension bridge. The bridge opened in 1929 and is 7,500 feet long. With more than 10,000 vehicles moving across it every day, it's one of North America's busiest international border crossings. Mostly made of steel (21,000 tons), it rises about 152 feet above the Detroit River.

Naming the Bridge

The bridge was going to be called simply the Detroit River Bridge. But Joseph Bower, who was paying most of the cost of the bridge, decided he wanted something different, so he renamed it the Ambassador Bridge to show the connection between two different countries. (An ambassador is a government official sent to represent one nation while living in another.)

Henderson Helped

On the American side, the McClintic-Marshall Company of Pittsburgh, Pennsylvania, was chosen to build the structure. (This company later built the Golden Gate Bridge in San Francisco.) On the Canadian side, Cornelius Henderson, a Black Detroiter, was one of the key players in designing and overseeing the installation of the steel sections. Henderson worked for the Canadian Bridge Company his whole life and also helped build the Detroit-Windsor Tunnel, which opened in 1930.

Cornelius Henderson

Outdoor Art in Detroit

Ask a Detroit local what their favorite outdoor work of art is, and you will receive a variety of responses. Along with the mighty *Spirit of Detroit*, you can choose from murals to fountains to sculptures.

James Scott Memorial On Belle Isle Park, you'll find this famous fountain, finished by creators Cass Gilbert and Herbert Adams in 1925. It features beautifully carved lions, turtles, and dolphins. The fountain can send water shooting 125 feet into the sky.

The Z Lot Art in a garage? Sure, why not!? This 10-story public parking garage houses 500,000 square feet of murals planned and executed by dozens of artists from across the world. It's at the intersection of Library Street and Gratiot Avenue.

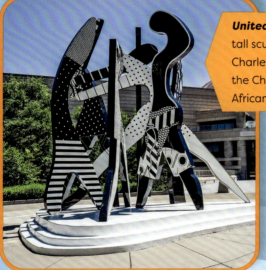

United We Stand This 20-foot-tall sculpture made by local artist Charles McGee stands in front of the Charles H. Wright Museum of African American History.

The Bear and the Boy This sculpture was made by Marshall Fredericks in 1954 for the J.L. Hudson Company. Made of limestone and bronze, it features a little boy riding a bear. It is displayed at the public library of Southfield, a northern suburb of Detroit.

Art in Museums

Do you love art? The Detroit Institute of Arts is the place to go! The DIA collection is considered one of the top six museums in the United States. It has more than 658,000 square feet of exhibition space and over 100 galleries. Make sure to check out the hands-on activities for kids and the Kresege Court for dining options!

Museum of Contemporary Art
MOCAD was opened in 2006 to expand Detroit's contemporary art community and help to nurture social change through art and exhibitions.

54 Detroit

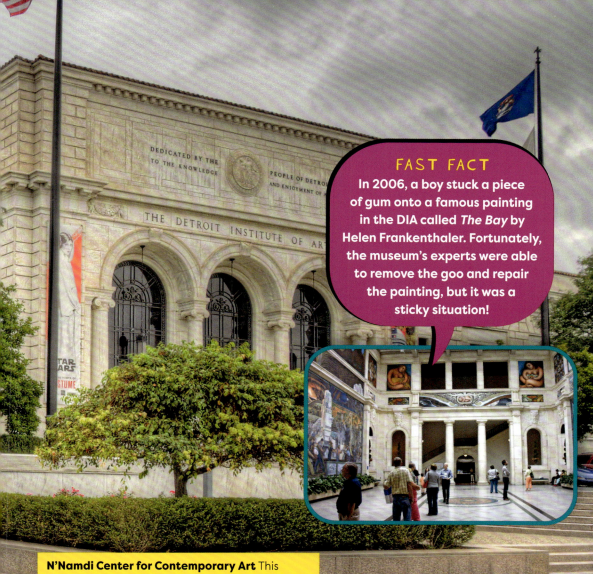

FAST FACT
In 2006, a boy stuck a piece of gum onto a famous painting in the DIA called *The Bay* by Helen Frankenthaler. Fortunately, the museum's experts were able to remove the goo and repair the painting, but it was a sticky situation!

N'Namdi Center for Contemporary Art This gallery is known as one of the most important modern abstract art galleries for local, national and international art from up-and-coming African American artists. George N'Namdi opened the Gallery in 1980 to raise awareness of abstract art and encourage a new generation of art collectors.

Red Bull Arts Detroit Red Bull primarily serves as an artist residency program for emerging artists, but they do have gallery hours where you can view pieces that their artists are currently working on.

Detroit 55

How to TALK Detroit

Detroiters, like residents of every other city on the earth, use a range of phrases that are understood primarily by the locals. Spend a day in Detroit and you will surely hear some of the following phrases.

Coney or Coney Island

In Detroit, it's both a restaurant and a beef hot dog on a bun with chili, mustard, and onions on top. (In New York, it's a place where people go to have fun at the beach.)

What up, doe?

This is how Detroiters say "Hello!"

Buffs

The nickname given to Cartier sunglasses, popularly worn in the City of Detroit.

"That's Bogue"
A slang word for bad. It comes from the word *bogus*.

The Cottage
This refers to one of the many log cabins in the Upper Peninsula of Michigan where Detroiters go for vacation.

Yuh Guys
Detroiters say "Yuh guys" instead of "y'all" or "you guys" when talking to groups of friends.

Michigan Left
Because of how some of Michigan's roads are made, people can't just turn left. At intersections where you can't turn left, there's a special lane for making U-turns. After that, they can turn right!

Detroit

DETROIT: It's Weird!

Hamtramck Disneyland You won't find Mickey, Donald, or Goofy here, but it's worth a visit to check out this remarkable folk art. Over many years, artist Dmytro Szylak built a wacky collection of found objects that form a massive sculpture. The name comes from the Detroit suburb where the structure was built; why Disneyland? Why not?

Marvin's Marvelous Mechanical Museum The collection of Marvin's Marvelous Mechanical Museum includes dozens of coin-operated games, animated machines, and other unique collectibles. It may be impossible to see everything in a single trip.

The Heidelberg Project You have to see it to believe it! In this neighborhood in the heart of Detroit's east side, a large-scale outdoor art installation features wonderfully painted houses, along with brilliant colors applied to abstract objects. It's a huge tourist attraction!

Octopus on Ice When the Detroit Red Wings hockey team wins a playoff game, a few fans toss a dead octopus onto the ice. The tradition started when it took eight victories (eight arms, get it?) to win a Stanley Cup title. The squishy tradition continues, though the team and animal rights folks continue to work to stop it.

PETA PS: Though this is a longstanding tradition, it's actually against Detroit law. Plus, fans can be thrown out and fined for throwing cephlapods. Plus, it's not very nice to the cephalopods, even if they are already dead. PETA (an animal rights group) has handed out little rubber octopi for fans to throw instead.

Detroit 59

Famous People Today

Kristen Bell, Actor
This TV and movie actor, known for her roles in "Veronica Mars", "Frozen," and "The Good Place," was born in Huntington Woods, a suburb to the north of Detroit.

Kenya Moore, Actor and TV host
Born in Detroit, Kenya is a multi-talented American celebrity who has worked as an actor, model, producer, writer, and TV host. She became famous after she competed in and won the 1993 Miss USA pageant and later starred in the Real Housewives reality show.

Jemele Hill, Sportswriter
Jemele was born in Detroit and started her sportswriting career at the *Detroit Free Press* newspaper. She moved on to work at ESPN for 12 years, where she hosted several shows and wrote for the ESPN website. She now covers sports for *The Atlantic* magazine.

Eminem, Rapper
Born Marshall Mathers (known as Eminem) in a Detroit suburb, he has become one of the most successful rappers of all time and is credited with spreading hip-hop to middle America. As a result of his huge popularity and rave reviews, Eminem is often praised with paving the way for white rappers to be included in the mainstream of hip-hop. He often features Detroit in his lyrics.

Detroit

What People Do in DETROIT

Metro Detroit is home to more than four million people. There are many different industries that keep the city of Detroit going. Here are a few of them.

Cars
Ford, Chrysler, and General Motors are together the biggest employers in Detroit and the state of Michigan. General Motors' world headquarters is located right near the Detroit riverfront.

Finance

Quicken Loans moved their headquarters to Downtown Detroit in 2010, and since then they have been growing quickly. Rocket Companies used to be the biggest mortgage company in the United States. Now, they have moved into other fields and are taking over and reviving more and more space in Downtown Detroit.

Shipping

Because it is on an international border, Detroit has always been known for its shipping and logistics (organizing how stuff moves around). Since this crossing is one of the busiest international crossings in North America, it gets busy and crowded really fast.

Healthcare

Detroit is home to world-class hospitals including Henry Ford Hospital, Hutzel Hospital, Detroit Medical Center, and others.

Detroit

Go, Detroit Sports!

Detroit fans LOVE their teams, filling stadiums and arenas to show their devotion.

DETROIT TIGERS

Joined Major League Baseball in 1901
Won Four World Series Championships, 1935, 1945, 1968, 1984
Big Names: Ty Cobb, Al Kaline, Justin Verlander, Miguel Cabrera, Lou Whitaker, Cecil Fielder
Home: Comerica Park

FAST FACT
- They played from 1912 to 1999 in famous Tiger Stadium. The stadium was demolished in 2009.
- The team's well-known D logo is in the Olde English style.

Detroit

DETROIT LIONS

Joined the National Football League in 1920
Won Four NFL championships (1935, 1952, 1953, and 1957)
Big Names: Barry Sanders, Ndamukong Suh, Mel Farr, Herman Moore, Matthew Stafford
Home: Ford Field

- The Lions have never won a Super Bowl.
- They once had a season in which they didn't win one game!

Detroit 65

DETROIT PISTONS

Began as the Fort Wayne Pistons in the Basketball Association of America; joined the NBA in 1949; moved to Detroit in 1957.
Won NBA title: 1989, 1990, 2004
Big Names: Joe Dumars, Isaiah Thomas, Ben Wallace, Chauncey Billups, Lindsey Hunter, Grant Hill, Bill Laimbeer
Home: Little Caesars Arena

The team's name comes from a part of a car's engine that makes it go! Yet another Motown car connection!

Isiah Thomas

The Detroit Shock played in the WNBA from 1998–2006, winning league championships in 2003, 2006, and 2008. The team moved to Tulsa in 2010 and to Dallas in 2016, where they play today as the Wings.

DETROIT RED WINGS

Joined the National Hockey League in 1926

Won The Stanley cup 11 times since 1936, most recently in 2008. It's the most championships by any American team in the NHL.

Big Names: Gordie Howe, Steve Yzerman, Alex Delvecchio, Sergei Fedorov, Ted Lindsay

Gordie Howe

The team's logo includes a car tire, a nod to the city's automotive industry.

Detroit

The Woodward Dream Cruise

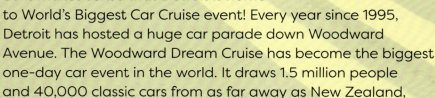

This is Motown, the City on Wheels, the biggest car city in the US, right? So it makes sense that Detroit is home to World's Biggest Car Cruise event! Every year since 1995, Detroit has hosted a huge car parade down Woodward Avenue. The Woodward Dream Cruise has become the biggest one-day car event in the world. It draws 1.5 million people and 40,000 classic cars from as far away as New Zealand, Australia, Japan, and Russia. North American cruisers from California, Georgia, Canada, and everywhere in between travel to Metro Detroit to take part in what has become an annual tradition for many. Spectators set up lawn chairs and grab snacks to watch the parade roll past. It's a Detroiter tradition!

68 Detroit

Other Annual Events

The Detroit Jazz Festival is one of the world's best. Since it was first held in 1980, the Jazz Festival has grown, drawing more than 2.5 million people each year to hear the best jazz musicians in the world.

Arts, Beats and Eats is an annual festival that draws over 300,000 people from all around the state and exhibitors from across the country. Arts, Beats, and Eats features the best art, music, and food from all over the state and country. It has been ranked as one of the best fine-art shows In the US.

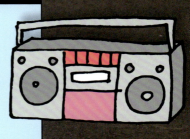

Detroit

COLLEGE TOWN

Detroit and several cities nearby are home to several important colleges and universities.

WAYNE STATE UNIVERSITY

Founded: 1868
Students: 27,222
Popular Majors: Psychology; International Business/Trade/Commerce; Biology/Biological Sciences; Public Health
FastFact: It began in 1868 as the Detroit Medical College. In 1934, it merged with other colleges in the city of Detroit to form the school it is today.

UNIVERSITY OF MICHIGAN, ANN ARBOR

Founded: 1817
Students: 44,718
Popular Majors: Computer and Information Sciences; Business Administration and Management; and Economics
FastFact: The state's oldest university, U of M began as a small school in Detroit founded by Father Gabriel Richard and others.

UNIVERSITY OF DETROIT MERCY
Founded: 1877
Students 5,227
Popular Majors: Nursing; Biology/Biological Sciences; Business Administration and Management; Engineering, Dental Hygiene.
FastFact: This is the largest Catholic university in Michigan.

MICHIGAN STATE UNIVERSITY
Founded: 1855
Students: 50,344
Popular Majors: Logistics, Engineering, Management, Marketing, Social Sciences, and Psychology
FastFact: Located in central Michigan, this school has a solar car racing team and an organic farm run by students.

EASTERN MICHIGAN UNIVERSITY
Founded: 1849
Students: 21,105
Popular Majors: Education, Business, Management, Marketing
FastFact: In Ypsilanti, due east of Detroit, this is the second oldest public university in Michigan.

Eat the Detroit Way

Detroit is known for its food as well as its cars. Let's dive in to see what kind of tasty treats we can try!

A paczki (pronounced POONCH-kee) is a type of donut that is deep-fried and filled with a sweet filling (usually jelly). Paczkis are originally from Poland, but there are also paczkis from German, Jewish, and Italian traditions.

Detroit Style Pizza was created by Gus Guerra and Concetta "Connie" Piccinato. They created the first crispy crust, square pizza in the United states. Detroit pizza is made with Wisconsin cheese, not mozzarella like Italian versions. The thick crust and square shape make it stand out as well.

Greek-inspired dishes like flaming cheese and pita bread are a staple with the city's large Greek population. Head to Greektown to enjoy those and other authentic Greek food.

The Mexican community in Detroit has been growing fast, so some of the state's best Mexican restaurants are found in Detroit. There is even a section of the city called Mexicotown!

Detroit is home to one of America's largest Arab American populations. This means a wide choice of eateries that serve tasty items like chicken kafta, fattoush salads, and chicken shwarma sandwiches.

Soda or Pop?

The oldest soda pop in the country is Vernors, created by accident in 1866. The term "pop" was created by another Detroit company called Faygo. It was coined after the sound the lid made when it popped off the soda bottle. So people in Detroit call sugary, bubbly drinks "pop."

DETROIT STREET QUIZ

There are hundreds of streets in Detroit with names that even trip up the locals. See how you do on this quiz to guess how to pronounce these street and place names in greater D-Town! (Hint: Just because it looks French, doesn't mean Detroiters say it with a French accent!)

1. Dequindre Street

Named after Antoine Dequindre, this runs north and south through Detroit.

2. Lahser Road

Named after Charles Augustus Lahser and heading north toward Bloomfield Hills.

Detroit

3. Cadieux
a famous Detroit French café.

4. Gratiot Ave
One of the main streets in Detroit.

5. Livernois
A suburb in northwest Detroit.

6. Schoenherr
A short street in northeast Detroit.

7. Hamtramck
This famous suburb of Detroit, to the north, gets its name from the Polish language.

Answers: 1. "duh-QUIN-durr," 2. LAH-sir 3. cad-JOU 4. GRAH-shut 5. LIV-er-noy 6. SHANE-er 7. ham-TRAM-ick

Detroit 75

We Saw It At The Zoo

The Detroit Zoo has more than 125 acres and houses more than 2,000 animals. The original zoo opened in 1928 and is visited by thousands of people every year.

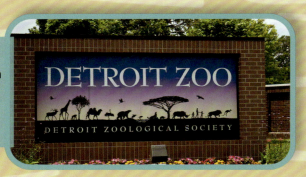

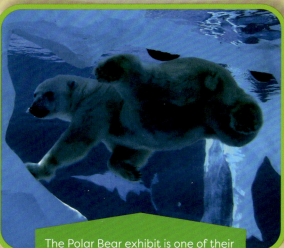

The Polar Bear exhibit is one of their most famous exhibits. It is a walk-through tunnel where you can see the polar bears swimming all around you, and is one of the largest polar bear habitats in North American.

At the Giraffe Encounter exhibit, you can feed these tall animals from an 18-foot platform!

There are 11 kangaroos and two wallabies in the Australian Outback exhibit.

Red kangaroo

Watch river otters dive and swim in a 9,000-gallon aquatic area, which features a sandy beach and a stream.

More than 75 penguins live at the Detroit Zoo. The Polk Penguin Conservation Center is the world's largest such place for penguins.

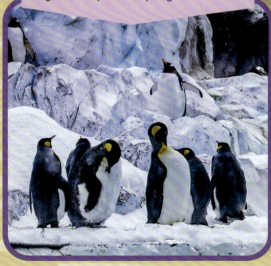

Detroit 77

It's Alive! Animals in Detroit

Even though Detroit is a city, there are still plenty of places for animals to live. With many areas of vacant land and the largest island park in the country, wildlife has a lot of choices. You can see these and other animals if you look carefully around the city.

Coyote

Beaver

Bald eagle

Pheasant

Peregrine falcon

Farm animals walking down Woodward Avenue are unusual, but not "unherd" of. In 2003, Jefferson, a young steer, got loose on his way to the Detroit Eastern Market. He ran miles through Detroit on some of the busiest streets in the city. After he was caught by police, the confused animal was sent to SASHA Farm to live out life in peace and quiet.

Detroit

BELLE ISLE PARK: THE JEWEL OF DETROIT

Belle Isle Park is one of Detroit's most popular tourist attractions and a popular destination for locals. America's largest city-owned island park, it has beaches, great views of the Detroit skyline, a golf course, a yacht club, a wildlife center, and much more!

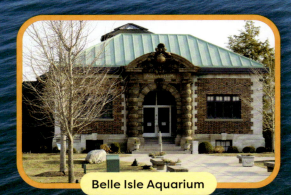
Belle Isle Aquarium

Belle Isle Conservancy

FAST FACT
The original name of Belle Isle Park was *Île aux Cochons* (Hog Island) and was changed to Belle Isle in 1845. The new name means beautiful island, so that was a nice upgrade!

Belle Isle Nature Center

Belle Isle Beach

Spooky Sites

Even if you don't believe in ghosts, going to scary places always sounds like fun. Let's take a look at these scary places in the Detroit area.

The Whitney: This mansion was built for lumber baron David Whitney Jr. between 1890 and 1894. It is said that the spirits of Whitney and his first wife, Flora, still live there. She always wanted to live in a mansion, but she died before the house was finished, leaving Whitney to raise their four children. Legend has it that the elevators occasionally work on their own!

Cadieux Cafe: Guests of the Cadieux Cafe have reported seeing the ghost of Yvonne Devos, the owner's late mother, sitting at the bar or at a table while gazing off into the distance.

Alhambra Apartements: Now abandoned, the building was the site of a 1905 double murder, and some say the victims haunt the hallways!

Haunting the Fords: Henry and Clara Ford lived in the Fair Lane estate until Clara died in 1950. Today, a ghostly butler is said to still be on duty! Spooky!

The Majestic Theatre: Some people say that the ghost of famous magician and escape artist Harry Houdini still haunts the Majestic, where he did one of his last shows.

Detroit

DETROIT BY THE NUMBERS

Stats and facts and digits . . . galore! Here are some of the numbers that make Detroit what it is.

755 FEET
Height of the city's tallest Skyscraper, the Detroit Marriott at the RenCen.

15.9 MILLION
people visit Detroit annually

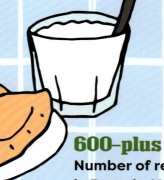

600–plus
Number of restaurants in Detroit. Yum!

Detroit

Number, Please
Detroit was the first city in the US to give people individual phone numbers, way back in 1879.

21 degrees F
Average low temperature in chilly January.

Seven
Pounds of potato chips Detroiters eat each year (on average), the highest number in the US.

308
Number of parks in the city.

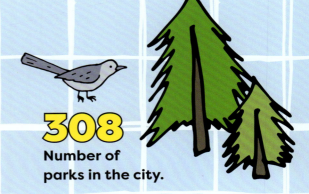

Detroit

Not Far Away

Detroit has plenty of things to do but in case you want to explore, here are some other great places in the area that are just a short drive away.

What up doe?! How is your trip going?

It's going great, we just got back from kayaking!

Kayaking? I thought you went to Detroit?

We did, and we decided to go visit **Mackinac Island** and do some exploring.

Oh how fun, I guess. How long did it take for you to drive there?

Mackinac is a car-free island, we had to take a ferry. But it took us about 4 hours to drive to the ferry.

Um . . . no cars?

Yes, it's horse drawn carriages and bikes only. We are staying at the **Grand Hotel**.

Wow that looks nice. That's a pretty big porch.

86 Detroit

> Yup, it's the longest front porch in the world. It's 660 feet!

That's a lot of resting

> We needed it after hiking up to **Arch Rock**. It was over 200 steps.

Whoa! That looks pretty steep!

> It was! Now time to get some fudge.

Ooh I love fudge! bring me some back!

> I will! Next up . . . **Skull Cave**!

Oh my gosh! Did you go in there?

> Nope! lol!

Detroit 87

> Earlier in the week we went to Tahquamenon Waterfalls, and it was gorgeous. It's literally Michigan's largest waterfall.

That's super cool. Seems like it would be cold though.

> Well it was a little cold, but the trees and wildlife were really nice!

I'm glad you're exploring and having fun, but what about the food?

> Oh my gosh, we had Coney dogs and Boston Coolers earlier this week.

You had a "who" and a "what?"

> A Boston Cooler! Vernors ginger ale and ice cream blended. And a Coney dog. An amazing hot dog with chili, onions, and mustard. It was so tasty.

Well, if you say so.

> Oh, I totally say so! it just all blends together!

Ok well back to the exploring . . . what else have you seen?

Detroit

> We decided to go to the Pictured Rocks National Lakeshore. The water was so pretty and blue.

Blue water? In Michigan?

> Yes! the hike was 11 miles along the cliff, but the view was so worth it!

I know you were exhausted after that!

> We sure were. the drive back was pretty long. but super beautiful. I don't think I'll ever forget how beautiful the trees were that lined the roads. They were even starting to change color.

Sounds like you were outside and around water a lot! Way more than I expected.

> Yes! Even when we were downtown Detroit. We decided to grab some ice cream and sit on the Riverwalk. We were literally looking at Canada!

Whoa! Talk about a close encounter!

Detroit 89

Sister Cities Around the World

Sisters are forever, right? Well, under the Sister Cities Program, the Motor City is connected to 11 cities across the globe.

Detroit's Sister Cities

Sister Cities in Action
Here are some examples of how Detroit is working with and helping its sister cities:

Dubai: The two cities linked up in 2003 to help build economic relationships. More than 300,000 Arab-Americans live in the Detroit area, one of the places in the United States with the most people with roots in the Middle East.

Toyota: While Detroit is the Motor City, one of Japan's Motor Cities is this one, home to (you guessed it) the Toyota Company. They've been sister cities since 1960, and students from Detroit and Toyota have swapped places every year for exchanges.

Minsk: Belarus is a country in Eastern Europe, and this is its capital. Detroit and Minsk have been sister cities since 1979.

Turin: Like Toyota, Turin and Detroit are linked as the places where cars are made. Turin is home to the famous Fiat company, which has been making cars since 1900. The Sister Cities program began here in 1998, and the cities have shared economic and educational programs.

INDEX

Ally Detroit Center 25
Ambassador Bridge 6, 7, 50-51
Arts, Beats, and Eats 69
Banks, Robert 19
Bell, Kristen 60
Belle Isle 38, 52, 80-81
Blackburns 18
Bower, Joseph 50
Cadieux Café 82
Cadillac, Antoine Laumet de la Mothe 10, 14
Campus Martius Park 36
Charles H. Wright Museum of African American History 29, 40, 53
Civil War 18, 20
Cooper, Alice 32
De Baptiste, George 19, 37
Detroit Anti-Slavery Society 19
Detroit Historical Museum 40
Detroit Institute of the Arts 29, 40, 54
Detroit Jazz Festival 69

Detroit Lions 65
Detroit Pistons 25, 66
Detroit Red Wings 25, 43, 59, 67
Detroit River 6, 10, 12-13
Detroit Shock 66
Detroit Tigers 24, 43, 64
Detroit Zoo 76-77
Dossin Great Lakes Museum 38
Eastern Market 39
Eastern Michigan University 71
Eminem 61
Finney, Seymour 19
Fisher Building 35
food 4, 28, 39, 69, 72-73
Ford, Henry 8, 22, 41, 62
Ford, Henry II 25
Ford Motor Company 4, 8, 9
Forth, Elizabeth 26
Franklin, Aretha 33
Fredericks, Marshall 42, 53
General Motors 4, 62
Gordy, Berry 24, 30
Great Fire 16

Hammond Building 21
Hart Plaza 36
Heidelberg Project 59
Henderson, Cornelius 51
Henry Ford Greenfield Village 41
Hill, Jemele 61
Houdini, Harry 83
Jackson 5 31
Jackson, Michael 31
James Scott Memorial 52
Kahn, Albert 29, 35
King, Charles Brady 22
King, Dr. Martin Luther Jr. 24, 31
Lake St. Clair 6
Knight, Gladys 31
Lambert, William 19
Lightfoot, Madison J. 19
Louis, Joe 26, 36
Mackinac Island 86-87
Majestic Theater 83
Malcolm X 27
Marvin's Marvelous Mechanical Museum 58
McCoy, Elijah 21

92 Detroit

Michigan State University 71
Michigan Science Center 40
Model T 9
MoGo 46
Monroe, Rev. William C. 37
Moore, Kenya 60
Motown 4, 24, 28, 30-31
Motown Museum 39
Museum of Contemporary Art 54
Nation of Islam 27
N'Namdi Center for Contemporary Art 55
North American International Auto Show 29
Northwest Territory 16
Olds, Ransom 8
Ojibwe people 14
Ottawa people 14
Parks, Rosa 27
People Mover 47
Pictured Rocks National Lakeshore 89

Polk Penguin Conservation Center 77
pizza, Detroit style 4, 72
QLine 47
Renaissance Center 35
Red Bull Arts Detroit 55
RiverWalk 12-13, 36
Rogers, Maj. Robert 16
Ross, Diana 33
St. James Episcopal Church Denison 26
Second Baptist Church 18, 37
Seven Years' War 15, 16
Sister Cities 90-91
street names 74-75
Spirit of Detroit 42-43, 52
Szylak, Dmytro 58
Tahquamenon Waterfalls 88
Underground Railroad 18-19, 36
University of Detroit Mercy 71
University of Michigan, Ann Arbor 70

Vernors Ginger Ale 5, 21, 88
Washington, Pres. George 17
Wayne, Gen. Anthony 17
Wayne State University 20, 70
weather 44-45, 85
Whitney, The 82
Windsor, Ontario 37
"The Wiz," 31
Wonder, Stevie 31, 32
Woodward, Augustus B. 17, 22, 36
Woodward Avenue 22, 24, 42, 46, 68, 78
Woodward Dream Cruise 68
WWJ 23
Young, Coleman 25
The Z Lot 53

Detroit 93

FIND OUT MORE!
Books, Websites, and More!

Books

Gregory, Josh. *Michigan: A True Book.* Scholastic, 2017.

Isgro, Bailey Sisoy. *Rosie, A Detroit Herstory.* Great Lakes Books, 2019.

Streissguth, Tom. *It's Great to Be a Sports Fan in Michigan.* North Star Books, 2022.

Tucker, Zoe. *Friends Change the World: We Are the Supremes.* Wide-Eyed Editions, 2021.

About the Author

Daralynn Walker, a native Detroiter, lives for the chance to express her creativity through the written word. Her children's book series, "Madison Miles and Friends," follows four young girls in Detroit who are passionate about science, technology, engineering, and math. She prefers to spend her free time reading, watching old TV shows, and spending time with her loved ones. Visit **www.madisonmilesandfriends.com** to learn more about her and The Madison Miles and Friends crew!

Web Sites

Detroit Science Center
https://www.detroitsciencecenter.org

Chelsea Treehouse
https://www.thechelseatreehouse.com

Cranbrook
https://science.cranbrook.edu

Ann Arbor Hands-On Museum
https://discoverscienceandnature.org

Photo Credits and Thanks

All photos from Dreamstime, Shutterstock, or Wikipedia, along with these sources: Alamy: Niday Picture Library 15B; TCD/Prod.DB 31B. AP Images: 24 bkgd; 24B; Doug Pizac 25C; Wilfredo Lee 58. Flickr: Chuck Anderson 52. Newscom: Amy Leang/Detroit Free Press 66B.

Artwork: Lemonade Pixel; Maps (6-7) by Jessica Nevins. Cover typography by Swell Type.

Thanks to our pal Nancy Ellwood, Jessica Rothenberg, and the fine folks at Arcadia Children's Books!